I lost summer somewhere

I lost summer somewhere

Poems by

Sarah Russell

Cover design by Shay Culligan
Cover art: "Autumn Tapestries" by Erin Hanson
www.ErinHanson.com

ISBN: 978-1-949229-79-0

Kelsay Books
Aldrich Press
www.kelsaybooks.com

For Roy Clariana
husband, lover, friend

with thanks to my fellow poets
in the State College Poetry Workshop,
to those who made suggestions along the way,
and to Ryan Stone, Aussie writing buddy extraordinaire.

Acknowledgments

Autumn Sky Poetry: The Day of the Eclipse

Goodreads Newsletter: Denouement (Goodreads contest
    winner). Republished in *Autumn Sky Poetry* and in
    WAVES: A Confluence of Women's Voices.

Black Poppy Review: Augury, Near the Tracks (published
    as Hegira)

Flutter Poetry Journal: Ricordo

Kentucky Review: Leaving West Virginia (Poetry Nook
    contest winner)

Misfit Magazine: Ravens

One Sentence Poems: On the Serengeti, Early Marriage

Poetry Breakfast: I lost summer somewhere, Maintenance,
    The Cottage

Poppy Road Review: Indian Summer, On Kebler Pass

Psaltery and Lyre: A Gospel of Birds (Pushcart nominee)

Red Eft Review: Ephemera

Right Hand Pointing: Learning to Play Baseball

Rusty Truck: After the Fact

Secrets and Lies: When I told truth to go away (published as
    The Secret)

Shot Glass Journal: At the Beauty Salon, Chancing Love,
    Rethinking Irina Dunn, Taxi

Silver Birch Press: If I Had Three Lives (Poetry Nook contest
    winner)

The Houseboat: Invitation, Sustenance

Third Wednesday: The Fold

Vita Brevis: Christmas Card

Word Fountain: Recurrence

Contents

III

IV

When I told truth to go away

we were girls—
blossom-cheeked,
skipping rope with life.
"I can't be your friend," I told her.
"You know my secret."
Truth shrugged. "OK.
I'll be here when you need me."
She waved goodbye, and went
to live in the hills
with hummingbirds and foxes.
I stayed behind, secure in my choice,
though joy was hard to find, I never
trusted love, and I reacted oddly
to the seemingly mundane—
lilies made me nauseous, Black Beauty
gave me nightmares, a breeze against my neck
could make me cry. After fifty years,
I looked for Truth again.
She hadn't changed—still young,
sweet, smiling, glad to see me.
But I'd become Wilde's portrait in the attic—
haggard, bitter, burden-stooped.
I asked what would have happened
if I'd let her have her way.
"You'd have suffered," she said. "People
would have shamed you. They'd say
you made it up. But you'd be free."

I

46 Catherine Street

I hid behind the Spirea bushes over there, by the steps,
chewed the bitter leaves, watched old Grandma Yonkers
in her lace-up shoes and cotton hose mince slow,
slow, with her squeak-wheeled shopping cart,
an hour to the store and back. She never saw me,
or at least she didn't say. The house is run down now.
Probably was then too, but kids don't notice shabby
when it's theirs. Screens are rusty, porch sags,
sidewalk buckled higher from the oak. Dad said
it should come out, but it's outlived him and will outlive
me as well. Its acorn caps made high-pitched squeals
between my thumbs I crooked just so. We raked
its leather leaves in piles at the curb, lit fires in the twilight,
watched embers spit into the blue black dusk—
the scent of autumn in my hair.

Where I grew up

there was a church across the street—
clapboard blistered, shingles curled.
Sundays, I saw girls
in mended hand-me-downs,
men in shiny-seated pants
and slicked back hair.
Holy Rollers, Mother called them.

Through open windows came
bellowed portents of perdition,
surging waves of rapture.
I sat on the stoop, arms clasped
around my knees, listening
from shore.

Christmas Card

My third Christmas,
Dad pulled the armchair
in front of the tree.
I sat on Mother's lap
with my favorite book.
Her gold crepe dressing gown
had fake leopard lapels.
I wore a nightie with flounces
and ribbons. Dad set up
the tripod and floodlights,
focused the Argus C-3.
Mother began to read.
I nestled so close
I could hear her heartbeat.
She got to the part,
"More rapid than eagles
his coursers they came . . ."
Dad had his shot,
turned the floodlights off.
Mother shut the book,
nudged me off her lap.

Near the Tracks

Those dream-filled summer nights,
it pierced the rusty screen—
a wail forsaken as a banshee.
Then the rhythmic clatter grew
until it shook the asphalt shingles,
until the bed and I would tremble.

Let me come too, I whispered,
but it never heard,
or didn't understand,
or didn't care about a little girl
and a gallant torn-eared bear.

The rumbling, shaking wraith
moved on, its cry waning to an echo,
my heartbeat clinging to the cadence
of *away from here, away from
here, away*

Late Epiphany

When all the kids went down
to Junie's basement the year
we turned thirteen, I stayed
to help her mother put candles
on the cake. I imagined
the spinning bottle, the dark
fruit cellar. I'd read *Peyton Place.*

A couple years later
after braces and Noxzema,
I tried it in the back seat of a Chevy
and came to Jesus.

Learning to Play Baseball

We were rounding third when I said
I love you. Not the look-deep-into-his-eyes
I love you. More a wow-this-feels-great
I love you. Turns out that's a foul ball
into the right field bleachers. Turns out
you can say mmmmmmmm or
ohgodohgod, but not . . . you know.

Leaving West Virginia

The road curls snug against the hills,
dips into hollows, rises up through stands
of oak, rough against dun clouds
that promise snow.

Old Jimmy waves goodbye, and Maude
is backlit in the door. Homesick starts here
on this gravel road, I guess—nuzzling deep
in sun-sweet quilts, an owl keeping himself company
at midnight, clanking the old stove to life
come morning.

The world is raw, waiting where the road
goes flat and blurs in the rush to get somewhere.
I watched for dawn this morning, breathless to be gone.
Now I want to salt away this place the way it is,
the way I was.

Chancing Love

Not a dive's precision arc.
Instead a lemming run and plunge,
oblivious to depth,
temperature, whether
water's in the pool.

Cynics shake their heads.
"Only a fool . . ." they say.
"Yes, yes!" I answer,
and drop my towel.

Michelin 5 Stars

We sat on the quai,
the Seine whispering by.
Your sweatshirt was our tablecloth,
my Swiss army knife, the silver.

A baguette,
saucisson,
a round of brie,
red wine with no label.

We fed each other strawberries,
fell in weekend love.

Live-in

I knew you'd leave eventually.
Easy come, easy go, I guess.
Mom always warned about giving
the milk away for free.

We never talked much
but it felt like home awhile—
a lonesome comfort,
another body taking up some space
so I didn't rattle.

When I got back from work today
your truck and stuff were gone.
I put on a pot of tea. You didn't warrant wine.
Besides, tea takes up more room.

Engagement

The sharp-edged city
softens in the snow.
Broken sidewalks calm
to undulations,
and street lights
dome a snow globe
for the scene below.
No wonder I said yes
when you proposed
and only later felt the cold.

II

Early Marriage

Our fights were a barrage of arrows
going to the softest places,
as if everything depended
on the outcome.

Sustenance

When glacial bogs blush with berries
it'll be a hard winter, folks say.

He is cutting down the dead pine near the cabin,
beetle-killed by drought last summer.
His chainsaw knows the hearth's width
without measuring.

I went to the orchard on Route 5
and bought peaches for canning.
The kitchen smells of sweetness,
furry skins sloughed off with blanching,
floor juice-sticky.

He comes in for lunch,
fills the room with flannel and sawdust.
"A lot of work," he says.
"Yes," I answer.
We eat warmed over stew. He cleans his plate
with bread crust and pushes back his chair.
"Back at it," he mutters and opens the door.

A cold wind makes gooseflesh on my arms
as I set the pint jars of preserves
in steaming water to make them sterile.

This forever place

… this clapboard house, these acres breathing deep
in August, Grandma's tidy rustling and hymns.
It's quiet in the parlor—a moth's wings against the screen,
the flutter of a tiny hand against my breast as I nurse.

A hundred years of memories crowd this room—
pastor visits, tea, Grandpa's viewing, carols around the piano,
the smell of balsam and camphor. Dust softens the outline
of the desk, tinges doilies and the Tiffany lamp. The rocker
creaks a lullaby. The baby murmurs as he sleeps,
his mouth milky at the corners.

Maintenance

Loose roof shingles—
a couple on the ground
after last night's wind
when the trees creaked
and rubbed themselves
like old men. Can't put off
the mending. I loved once,
before I knew how love
works, how roofs leak
when it rains.

Augury

I stopped for groceries after work.
Jeff will be late again tonight.
"Don't wait up," he always says.

I hate these country roads at dusk—
twisting, full of ruts. I woke
this morning choking back a scream,
but the dream escaped
with the trembling.

I round a bend, see movement
in the willows. Slow, I tell myself.
It's probably nothing.

Yokogami-yaburi

is Japanese for tearing paper
against the grain—
like that article you want to keep
but don't wait for scissors
and rip into the story so the gist
is lost, or being stuck at 40
in living-the-dream, left holding the bag
of groceries or laundry or dirty diapers,
so you hide your stretch marks in a one-piece,
toss your hair like Farrah, and smile at strangers
on the beach while the kids make sand castles,
or open a bottle at 10 a.m., or shop for things
you'll hide when you get home so when he asks
in two weeks you can say, "Oh, this old thing,"
or spend the afternoon online with men
who suggest a motel tryst—men whose photos
look suspiciously like the guy on page 34 of GQ—
just to see how far you can tear against the grain
before the gist is lost.

On the Serengeti

we watch a lioness charge back
to guard a week-old kill from jackals
and raw-necked buzzards
though she has long since had her fill.
As others photograph the scene,
you and I hold hands, knowing well
the desperate defense
of what is dead.

Invitation

We found a stream that night
away from everywhere but us—
water voices whispering the honey of first times,
the wind's breath feathery on urgent skin.

Perhaps a folly, our rush into
together and tomorrow—
forever's promissory note
before the debt of everyday.

Let's go back
and lie beside the stream again,
listen for the water voices,
feel the wind's breath

before we disappear.

Ephemera

I sit at the water's edge,
draw circles in the sand.
It was almost too civil. Last night
we walked down the beach
to the crab shack,
tied bibs around our necks,
and over a bucket of clams and corn
decided who got what.
Circles, short-lived in the tide,
my wedding ring in the dresser drawer.

Denouement

The movers are here this morning.
Only things with yellow post-its,
I tell them. I find my long lost earring
behind the couch. Probably landed there
that night we couldn't wait to get upstairs.
I put it in my pocket, wonder
if I kept the other one.

I divide the sterling service for eight
into two sets of four—
Solomon solution of no use
to either of us for dinner parties. Outside,
the garden needs tending—stalks of gray and brown,
withered blossoms in a winter without snow.
I reach for the pruners, then put them back.
The roses are his now.

Tonight I fix a curry with stuff from the fridge,
and we make small talk—my new job, his vacation.
Afterwards, we clean up in choreography
perfected through twenty years of meals together.

I feign tiredness and ask if he'll be around
tomorrow before I leave.
No, there's an early meeting, he says
and turns back to TV. In the guest room,
the sheets smell stale. The old cat comes
and curls into the crook of my knees—
an exquisite kindness.

After the Fact

There's the Fact,
and After the Fact—
the silence of a new apartment,
hugging the kids too hard,
watching them manipulate.
It's his telling friends you took him
to the cleaners, cold stares
at soccer games.

After the fact is buying hundred dollar jeans,
then eating ramen for a week,
lying about your age,
your weight.
It's wondering if they're mama's boys
or gays still in the closet,
what to do with small talk,
stretch marks. It's settling
for a 6 because you're horny.

The Fact's a piece of cake.

Swiss Cheese

Some days I catch myself making a sandwich
for him to take to work. I still buy Swiss cheese
though he's the one who liked holes.

On my fuck-him days, I take a slice, jam my finger
through a hole and twirl it 'til it tears and flies off.
Sometimes I let it lie on the floor collecting dog hair
and crumbs. Sometimes, I throw it away.

Rethinking Irina Dunn

"A woman needs a man
like a fish needs a bicycle,"
she said, and I concurred.
But this morning, Howard,
who always seemed happy
with his castle and plastic algae
asked me for a lift
to the Schwinn dealership,
and I said, "Hang on.
I'll grab my keys."

That night

you tore at silk
to empty your loneliness
into mine.
We slept tangled
in each other's scent,
woke
still strangers.

Taxi

I'm in a taxi at the end of nowhere,
meter running, searching for that place
I saw once when you loved me. The night
is an egg—thick, with a broken moon.
Since you've gone, I rack up days
like billiard balls, scatter them
to the corners, looking for a pocket—
any warm pocket.

III

Things that are real

babies crying at 2 a.m.
dust
the one you can't forget
the smell of rain
make believe
mosquitos
a kaleidoscope of autumn leaves
bullets
making love
a dog's loyalty
birth
a friend I trust

Lynn

I danced on Broadway, you said.
I know, I said. I stroked
your hair while you threw up
and only bile was left to feed
the fetus. They found the mess
of you in your car, though
you didn't like messes.
Your note came in the mail.

Some women refuse to live
a life of shit and string beans,

it said. I wish I'd known, I said.
I should have known.

Return

They're burning fields on the delta—
violent end of harvest.
Smoke billows above charred stubble,
chokes and blinds me as I drive.

Mom turns ninety on Sunday.
The whole town's invited
at two for cake and to say
how good she looks.

In truth, she's not good.
Fragile with diabetes, eyes failing,
fingers gnarled to claws;
no quilts for new babies.

Hard-willed as the life she's led,
she stays alone with a cat and a walker.
Folks look in on her from time to time, say
they'll let me know if something happens.

I've burned fields too.
College-trained for work not at the whim
of subsidies and drought, I expect
no feast for this prodigal.

Recurrence

"Here, feel this," is how it started
that morning she stopped by
like always Thursday mornings,
like always for tea and then we'd walk
along the river.

She lifted her arm, and I touched
the pale softness, knew
it was real, not maybe—
a hard currant of a thing.

"I want to live," she said,
and this time I knew
she didn't mean forever.

Supplicant

At the Cathedral of St. Anthony,
guardian of the lost,
I light a candle, pray for you—
not because I believe,
but because I am helpless.

I set aflame my worry
from another worry's flame—
burn wax and wick, my plea
reduced at last to soot
in a bed of sand, hoping
for saint or god or angel's wingspan
wide enough to shelter flickering souls.

A Gospel of Birds

She wasn't sure about heaven,
but she believed in birds.
On walks she'd stop to watch
a skein of geese, wondered
where they came from,
where they were heading.
They mate for life, she'd say.
Crows do too. And swans
and storks. She must have said that
a hundred times, with a kind of wonder
at the impossibility.

She kept five feeders on the deck,
had a book of backyard birds
to identify newcomers at the feast.
She cried when a neighbor's cat
killed a mourning dove. They mate
for life too, she said. Listen,
her mate is sad. That's just their call,
I told her. No, it's different, she said.
You can tell when birds are sad.

She died a month ago.
I keep the feeders filled.

Choice

I sat beside my daughter, held her hand
while a doctor probed and scraped
on the far side of the curtain.

Her grip was tight, a last clinging
to a shared innocence.
Neither of us cried.

"The baby would be in college now,"
she said to me the other day.
"I know," I said.

Ravens

The smartest man I know is dying—
cancer, spreading to his bones
and cruelly, to his brain.
"Come look back here,"
he says when I visit.
"They knew even before I did."

Six ravens walk—stately, slow, with purpose
across his yard—an avian funeral cortège.
"They've been here since spring," he adds.
 He points to a corner near the fence.
"That one has a broken wing. Got it
robbing a blue jay's nest.
Shouldn't mess with jays, I told her."

He feeds her raw chicken and steak,
but says that soon she'll ask
for death, and he'll oblige.
"They won't do the same for me.
Fucking do-gooders."
I don't know what to say.

"When she's gone, her fellows will have
a feast of her carcass," he says,
"just as they will with mine."
I try to protest, but I know it's true.
Already there's talk that his research is passé.

At lunch I see my reflection in a soup spoon.

The Day of the Eclipse

Leaves patchwork a trail to the stream.
My footfall on the bank scatters trout
who come to spawn each August, jeweled
reflections following instinct.
My son called today, a should-he
or shouldn't-he conversation. I listened,
questioned. His indecision is unknown
by wild things who live the primordial,
the insatiable.
Through the trees, moon eclipses sun
in an eerie twilight not ruled by manners,
mores, norms. Crickets start reverberations
in the trees. Bright glints in the water move
through my shadow, the moon's shadow—
stars in an ancient galaxy.

Past Tense

I didn't go to the funeral. "I'll need you more
later," she said. Now, a month into her widowhood,
she's fragile, desperately controlled.
"Look at that ding in the windshield,"
she says as we drive from the airport.
"I had it fixed so it wouldn't spread,
but it still shows."

We visit the cemetery on the way home.
She fusses because rain has softened the earth
around his grave, leaving it pockmarked, muddy.
"By next year, the grass will fill in," I say, hoping
it's OK that the outline where the coffin lies
will go away; hoping that's what she wants.
The shiny new marker has both their names,
like she's buried there already.

We pull into her driveway, and she points to a sign
on her golf-green-worthy lawn. "I got 'Yard of the Month'
this month," she says. "Seems like digging in the dirt
and dead-heading are all I do these days."

Ricordo

In Conca dei Marini, I visit
our favorite café at the water's edge,
order a glass of verdicchio,
watch light crystals play among the waves,
feel the breeze flirt with the hem
of my skirt, my hair. I remember
the word *culaccino*—the water mark
left by a glass sweating with cold
in the sun—and wonder how long
it will take the ring to disappear.

The Fold

The corners of death fold us into ourselves.
—Loretta Diane Walker

Mother and I are sniping. This visit
has been that way. The farm is rundown
as she is now at 94, bent over her walker,
bare-knuckled in her independence.
She says I mumble. I say she never listens.
We know this game. I'm packing to go home,
and she calls, "Do you want breakfast?"
I mutter yes, knowing she won't hear.
It starts again.

I'm her favorite and visit least. I'll look back
on this weekend, feel guilt. She will win
another round. This time when we hug goodbye,
there are no tears. As I drive away I glance
back to make sure she's still in the doorway,
watching.

IV

The Wisdom of Wonderland

Alice: How long is forever?
White Rabbit: Sometimes just one second.
                           —Lewis Carroll

You think it was just you who fell
that afternoon in Memphis.
But when I saw a lonely man,
nursing a beer at a Midtown bar
I knew I was seeing a lifetime.
I just didn't tell you until now,
a quarter century later, because
I had to learn to trust first.

Home

Late afternoon in the valley, the trees
wear halos. Then twilight steals the sun,
kitchen lights blink on like fallen stars,
and coming home is a sigh
and the smile of someone waiting.
Your day is told in half sentences
and nods and questions answered—
nothing new, but new enough to tell again.
After supper, after gin rummy and pages
turning and the rhythmic click of a sweater
growing row by row, bed greets you
like a childhood friend, and sleep
keeps company with the blue black sky
and the owl's whispered flight.

Indian Summer

I hike the ridge on the last warm, tousled day,
speckled as a partridge egg, sun already stilting
shadows in early afternoon. The leaves
are October butterflies, crimson, gold.
I want to stop earth's tilt-a-whirl right here,
hold this moment that feels so much like love
before the wind hones winter's blade.

Old Cottonwoods

Old cottonwoods turn silver as they die.
Sentinels of the plains, they are more constant
than a dowser conjuring water beneath the prairie's
grassy tide. In May their seeds loft in downy clouds,
find purchase in loam soft with spring,
then suffer August droughts, December gales.
When their century's watch is through
they shed their rough brown coats,
reach argent fingers toward the moon,
and hear a night bird's murmured elegy.

The Cottage

I've grown quiet here. My mind
has opened to woodsong
and the smell of earth turned
by a trowel.

I enjoy solitude, even when regrets
and the throb of an old lover happen by.
Sometimes I invite them in, make
a ritual of teacups on starched linen,
a silver server for the scones.
We reminisce 'til shadows trace
across the floor, call them away.

Afterwards, I tidy up, wipe away
drops spilled in the pouring. I save
the leftovers though they're getting stale.
I may crumble them on the porch rail
tomorrow for sparrows
before I garden.

At the beauty salon

I lean back and close my eyes
as a young woman washes my gray,
thinning hair. She massages in
shampoo, gently rubs my temples,
smooths the cream rinse—scented
with lavender—from my brow, and you
are here with me again that summer day
under the waterfall.

Old Lovers Meet

We hug, for a moment
catch each other's hand,
remembering the cadence
of shared dances.

We speak of children,
grandchildren, spouses,
but our eyes see butterflies
with battered wings
and transience
before the rain.

In my 70s

there's little time left
to see first tulips,
find tiny purple shells
still hinged, rake leaves
pungent with dying,
stoke the fire when wind
curls around the pane.

The novel in my head
has only time to be
a poem without last lines
to tell the reader
if she learned to love
the baby, if what the gypsy
said came true, if the letter
was from him.

On Kebler Pass

dust the ferns with my ashes—
there, among the aspen
trembling gold against the sky.
Let them settle, sighing,
on the still warm earth of autumn
where the next peak calls your name.

Snow will come. The wind will show me
paths known to the doe and vixen.
The moon will call me with her crescent mouth
and share stories of the embered stars.

About the Author

Sarah Russell has returned to poetry after a career teaching, writing and editing academic prose. She holds a Ph.D. in Communication Theory from the University of Colorado. Her poems have been published in *Kentucky Review, Red River Review, Misfit Magazine, Third Wednesday, Psaltery and Lyre,* and many other print and online journals and anthologies. She has won awards from Goodreads, Poetry Nook, and is a Pushcart Prize nominee. This volume of poetry received an Honorable Mention for the 2018 Concrete Wolf Louis Award. She lives in State College, Pennsylvania, with her husband Roy Clariana. They spend summers in Colorado to be near children and grandchildren. She blogs at: *SarahRussellPoetry.net.*

Made in the USA
Coppell, TX
11 February 2023

12648745R00049